D0926801

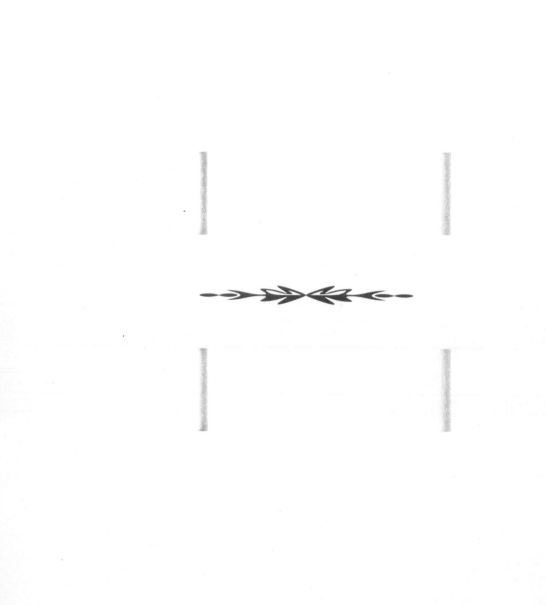

Jorge Mario Bergoglio

POPE
FRANCIS

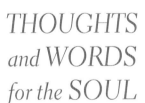

*THOUGHTS
and WORDS
for the SOUL*

WHITE STAR PUBLISHERS

WS White Star Publishers® is a registered trademark
property of De Agostini Libri S.p.A.

© 2014 De Agostini Libri S.p.A.
Via G. da Verrazano, 15
28100 Novara, Italy
www.whitestar.it - www.deagostini.it

Translation: Irina Oryshkevich

All rights reserved. No part of this publication may be reproduced, stored
in a retrieval system or transmitted in any form or by any means, electronic,
mechanical, photocopying, recording or otherwise, without written permission
from the publisher.

ISBN 978-88-544-0837-1
 2 3 4 5 6   18 17 16 15 14

Printed in Poland

TEXTS EDITED BY
GIUSEPPE COSTA

TEXTS OF THE HOLY FATHER
COURTESY OF THE
LIBRERIA EDITRICE VATICANA

PHOTOGRAPHS
FROM THE PHOTO ARCHIVES OF
L'OSSERVATORE ROMANO

FRANCISCUS

13TH MARCH 2013

ANNUNTIO VOBIS GAUDIUM MAGNUM;
HABEMUS PAPAM:

EMINENTISSIMUM AC REVERENDISSIMUM
DOMINUM,
DOMINUM GEORGIUM MARIUM
SANCTAE ROMANAE ECCLESIAE
CARDINALEM BERGOGLIO
QUI SIBI NOMEN IMPOSUIT FRANCISCUM

I announce to you a great joy:
WE HAVE A POPE!
The Most Eminent and Reverend Lord,
Lord Jorge Mario
Cardinal of the Holy Roman Church Bergoglio,
Who takes for himself the name Francis

PREFACE

Many books have been published on Pope Francis. Is there a place for this one? I think so, if we do not demand that it be anything more than a publication: a quick bird's eye view of the life of Pope Francis, a lot of photographs, several dozens of his opinions, excerpts of his speeches and teachings.

Certainly a Catholic Pope in a jeep who seems to be on an obstacle course through St. Peter's Square as he enthusiastically greets volunteers, children and the sick is an utter novelty. Even Elton John has been so taken by this Pope that he described him in *Vanity Fair* as "a miracle of humility in the age of vanity."

Pope Francis communicates with eloquent gestures and effective, direct language. His discourse touches listeners personally, provoking questions and exciting imagination through reference to collective memory and recourse to symbols. He communicates with his entire body, recalling McLuhan's expression, "the medium is the message." Surely we can state that he stands as substitute to the medium. Is this his strategy? It is difficult to say. Clearly he looks you in the eye, giving you a solid feeling that he is here to listen to you; he squeezes your hand and embraces you with feeling, exuding a sense of extraordinary accessibility, then takes his leave with a "pray for me, I need it," leading to the surrender of anyone with the good fortune and grace to meet him. His face, restrained and pensive during morning Mass yet joyful when encountering the public, and his voice, capable of railing against vice but also, like that of a new John the Baptist, of crying out loud the hopeful message of the Gospels, have not gone unnoticed by the media.

This publication – a mix of images and words – can be read or examined in detail. It can also make us think about a Church, a real site of encounter capable of adjusting itself to new criteria by renewing its crews and above all the eternal call of Christ: Come, I will make you the fishermen of men; lighten your loads and let us walk towards Resurrection.

INTRODUCTION

On the evening of March 13th, 2013, I found myself in St. Peter's Square. The definitive white plume of smoke was being said to be a possibility. When the announcement came that Jorge Mario Bergoglio had been elected, a noticeable sense of surprise filtered through the Square. In reality, many Italians had been expecting the election of Cardinal Scola, while Americans were betting on Dolan, Archbishop of New York, and Asians hoping for a Filipino or Indian. Afterwards, the choice of the name Francis immediately brought to mind a period of great religious awakening, such as that of the Assisi *Poverello*, but also the era of the great missionary campaigns, such as those of the Jesuit Francis Xavier

But who is this Pope Francis?

He was born in Buenos Aires on December 17th, 1936, in a city where life was punctuated by huge waves of Italian immigrants seeking fortune and wealth against the melancholic and romantic background music of Gardel's tango.

His father came from Piedmont, from Portacomaro (Asti), disembarking in Argentina from the *Giulio Cesare* in January 1929. His mother, Regina Maria Sivori, was born in Buenos Aires. The two were married on December 12th, 1935.

The father, an accountant, found work with the railroad, while the mother devoted herself to her five children: Oscar Adrian, Alberto Horacio, Marta Regina (all deceased), Maria Elena and Jorge Mario (still alive). "At that time our family was experiencing some economic difficulty, but we weren't starving to death," said the Pope's sister, Maria Elena Bergoglio, in an interview. "Moreover, I often heard my father say that the power of the fascists had actually caused their flight from the country."

As a child, Jorge lived in the atmosphere of Buenos Aires where he met the Salesians, in whose school he learned to love Our Lady Mary Help of Christians, the Eucharist, and the Pope, and also soccer and the San Lorenzo de Almagro team.

"He was a normal kid," recalls Maria Elena, "well-mannered and a good student; he always protected me because I was the youngest."

If with his father he often played cards and went to the stadium, with his mother – who became a paraplegic after her fifth pregnancy – Jorge used to listen to lyrical music broadcast over the public radio. From her he also acquired the habit of peeling potatoes and learned how to cook. He likewise spent much time with his grandmother Rosa, from whom he learned ancient wisdom and religious practices.

The adolescence of the future Pope was occupied not only with study but also with minor jobs for third parties, and there was no lack of anxiety and emotion. "He was always in the mood to joke around and was gallant," explained his childhood sweetheart Amalia Damonte, grey-haired and bespectacled today. "Our families were not happy about our friendship, but it was a very innocent thing; we were mere children."

He regularly went to mass near the harbor district of Flores. He received a diploma as a chemical technician in an Argentina that was in the process of development and a state of unrest. Classical learning, his father believed, would have been of no use to him.

Argentinian Catholicism was very lively during Bergoglio's adolescence. The International Eucharistic Congress presided by Cardinal Eugenio Pacellii, who was to become Pope in 1939, took place in 1934. The Church was engaged in widespread Catholic activity as all types of groups and associations were flourishing.

After graduating as a chemical technician, young Jorge turned to the priestly life, entering the diocesan seminary of Villa Devoto on the outskirts of the capital.

On March 11th, 1958, he passed on to the novitiate of the Company of Jesus and underwent the intense training course of the Jesuits. He completed his studies in Chile, and in 1963 returned to Argentina, where he received a degree in philosophy from the Colégio Máximo di San Miguel. Between 1964 and 1965 he taught literature and psychology at the Colégio de la Imaculada in Santa Fé, and in 1996 he moved on to the Colégio del Salvador in Buenos Aires.

From 1967 to 1970 he studied theology, and on December 13th, 1969, was ordained a priest. He was then sent to complete his training in Spain, where he professed his Perpetual Vows to the Jesuits. His Jesuit training impressed him profoundly.

As Pope, he declared on July 28th, 2013: "I feel myself to be a Jesuit in my spirituality, in the spirituality of the Exercises, which I hold in my heart." As Giandomenico Mucci S.J. wrote in the journal *La Civiltà Cattolica*, "It is natural that the Pope, who spent much of his youth and early adult life and entered the priesthood in the Company, feels himself to be a disciple of Ignatian spirituality. It is equally natural that his sermons resound with its great themes. Nonetheless this is not a minor aspect of his personality or sermons that would have remained hidden from the general public had the Pope himself not spoken about it. In the interview granted to the editor of our magazine, he described St. Ignatius not as an ascetic who led a silent and penitential life, but as a mystic. This view, bearing the weight of the experience and authority of the man who uttered it, is clearly opposed to the secular misrepresentation of the work and figure of the founder, whom literature, painting, and polemicists have usually been content to represent as a somber sixteenth-century ascetic of the Counter Reformation. The historic role played by the Company as well as the biased interpretation later given it by the Enlightenment, may have contributed to all this."

But why did Bergoglio become a Jesuit?

In the interview with the editor of *La Civiltà Cattolica*, Antonio Spadaro, he replied: "I wanted something more. But I didn't know what. I entered the seminary. I liked the Dominicans and I had Dominican friends. But later I chose the Company, which I knew well because the seminary was entrusted to the Jesuits. Three things about the Company struck me: their missionary work, sense of community and discipline. This is a curious thing because I was an undisciplined child by birth. But their discipline, their method of organizing time, moved me a great deal."

"And also, what is really essential to me is community. I was always looking for a community. I did not see myself solely as a priest: I needed a community. And this can be understood from the fact that I am here at Santa Marta. When I was elected, I was living in Room 207,

appointed to me by lot. The one we are in now was a guest room. I chose to live here, in Room 201, because when I took possession of the papal aparment, I felt within me a distinct 'no.' The pontifical apartment in the Apostolic Palace is not luxurious. It is old, decorated in good taste and large, not luxurious. But ultimately, it is like an overturned bottle-neck. It is large and spacious, but the entrance is really narrow. One enters as if through an eye dropper, and I – no – I cannot live without people. I need to live my life together with others."

On July 31st, 1973, Father Jorge Mario Bergoglio was elected Provincial Superior of the Jesuits of Argentina and held that post until 1979. Among his first decisions was to have the Jesuits withdraw from Salvador University in Buenos Aires.

After completing his six-year term as Provincial Superior, he once again became Rector of the Colégio Máximo and parish priest of a new parish, San Giuseppe in San Miguel, about twenty miles away from the federal capital.

In March 1986, he traveled to Germany and spent a short time attending the lectures of some professors at the prestigious graduate school of the Sankt Georgen Seminary in Frankfurt as well as in the Guardini Archive in Munich above all to expand his views on his philosophical work, *Der Gegensatz* (Contraries in Opposition). Upon his return, he was sent to the Colegio del Salvador of Buenos Aires and afterwards to the church of the Company in Córdoba as spiritual director and confessor.

Experience with the Church and Argentine society often emerges in the language of the present Pope. According to Father Scannone, his friend and teacher, "The manner of doing theology in Argentina owes much to the cultural climated created by Peronism. On a political level, Peronism granted great importance to workers, the famous *descamisados*, that is, the masses of laborers from the inland that merge in Buenos Aires. According to the Peronist concept, it is people not classes that are of great importance. People are understood and felt to be a category; as in Marxism, they are believed to arise from unity, not conflict. The "theology of the village" was born in Argentina, and some, like Gustavo Gultiérrez and I myself, consider it a current with its

own characteristics within Liberation Theology, though others distinguish it as something apart. It emerges from the unity among people to resolve conflict, not from class struggle. In Marxism, unity occurs only at the end, in the classless society. It is interesting that Bergoglio betook himself to Germany in order to analyze "contraries in opposition" in the thought of Romano Guardini, whom he held in great esteem. Gustavo Gultiérrez himself, founder of Liberation Theology, one day confessed to me that he saw in Peronism a niche outside of Marxism for those who fought for the poor. "I recall some firm points in Bergoglio's thinking: the whole is more than the sum of its parts; unity vanquishes conflict; reality carries more weight than ideas; time prevails over space."

In 1992 he was named Auxiliary Bishop of Buenos Aires.

Six years later, on February 28th, 1998, he was named Archbishop of the city and three years after that, on February 21st, 2001, he was created Cardinal by John Paul II.

In 2005, he took part in the conclave that elected Benedict XVI. Bergoglio received the votes of those who were opposed to Ratzinger.

Returning to Argentina, Cardinal Bergoglio devoted himself to the pastoral care of his diocese, granting particular importance to the exercise of charity and solidarity. Then, continuing a task already initiated by the Superior of the Argentine Jesuits, he worked on liberating and assisting the victims of the military dictatorship. Without Bergoglio's protection, not a few of the prisoners would have ended up on the list of *desaparecidos* [those who had disappered] – a list much longer than the Pope himself can remember.

In his two mandates as President of the Episcopal Conference of Argentina and as President in 2007 of the committee preparing the final document of the Fifth General Assembly of the Episcopal Council of Latin America (CELAM) in Aparecida, Brazil, he broadened his knowledge of the problematics of the relationship between the Church and Latin America. In terms of Aparecida, the general theme of which was "Disciples and missionaries of Jesus Christ, so that our people may have life in him," one can highlight six basic concerns present in the mind and heart of Pope Francis:

✣ to realize the biblical spirit in all pastoral work

✣ to bring to fullness the life of the people through participation in the Sunday Eucharist

✣ to renovate all church structures so that they are essentially of a missionary nature

✣ to reaffirm the option for the poor and the excluded

✣ to grow in a style of cordial proximity with the people

✣ to encourage everyone's obligation towards public life

In terms of the writings of Cardinal Bergoglio/Pope Francis, beyond his explicit references to documents, he captures the concordance of attitudes, practices and the dynamics of the Latin American and Caribbean Conference with the clarity of daylight.

In particular:

✣ in the methodology regarding the pastoral approach to reality (starting from real, concrete situations rather than from doctrinal principles and definitions, illuminating them with the light of the Gospels and proposing concrete courses of action)

✣ in the insistence on a not "self-referential" Church, which flows out not only to the geographical but also the "existential" periphery, where the poor, the most marginal and the excluded are found.

✣ in the concrete proposition (though not literally expressed) of the duo "communion and participation," which strives towards the elimination of all egoistic hoarding of either material goods or power, culture or social privilege by any individual or group, and towards the abolition of every form of marginalization and exclusion.

Since March 13th, 2013, Pope Bergoglio has committed himself to reforming and restoring to health the Vatican Curia. Communications of the eight cardinals presided by Cardinal Óscar Rodríguez Maradiaga have helped him identify those reforms that will relaunch the spiritual life of the Church and of Catholics. Because Pope Bergoglio is one who, starting from the certainty of a God who loves and stands for mercy, inspires hope. As Bishop of Rome he appeals to those who believe and those who do not, stretching out full circle, driving himself to being the protagonist of his own history and responding with responsibility to the call of God.

THOUGHTS AND WORDS FOR THE SOUL

*And now, we take up this
journey: Bishop and People.
This journey of the Church
of Rome which presides
in charity over all the
Churches.
A journey of fraternity,
of love, of trust among us.
Let us always pray
for one another.
Let us pray for the whole
world, that there may be a
great spirit of fraternity.*

God is not something vague. Our God
is not a "spray." He is tangible;
he is not abstract but has a name:
"God is love." His is not a sentimental,
emotional kind of love but the love of the
Father who is the origin of all life, the love
of the Son who died on the Cross and is
raised, the love of the Spirit who renews
human beings and the world.

We must not be afraid of being Christian and living as Christians! We must have this courage to go and proclaim the Risen Christ, for he is our peace, he made peace with his love, with his forgiveness, with his Blood and with his mercy.

Today let us not forget the love of God, the love of Jesus:
he watches us, he loves us, he waits for us.
He is all heart and all mercy.
Let us go with faith to Jesus; he always forgives us.

God's face is the face of a merciful father who is always patient. Have you thought about God's patience, the patience he has with each one of us? That is his mercy. He always has patience, patience with us, he understands us, he waits for us, he never gets tired of forgiving us if we are able to return to him with a contrite heart.

*To cross the threshold of faith entails having eyes that marvel and
a heart not accustomed to laziness, capable of realizing that each
time a woman brings a child to light, a gamble on its life and future
continues to be taken, that when we show concern for the innocence
of children, we guarantee the truth of the future, and when we cherish
the dedicated life of an aged person, we perform a just act
and nurture our roots.*

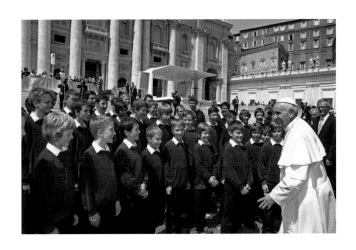

The look of love neither discriminates nor relativizes because
it is the look of friendship. And friends are accepted as they
are, and to them one tells the truth. It is also a communal look.
It urges one to keep company, to join oneself, to be one among
many while next to other citizens.
This look is the basis of sociable friendship, of respect for
difference, not only of the economic but also of the ideological
kind. It is also the basis of all volunteer work.
He who remains excluded cannot help himself if inclusive
communities are not created.

Here I would add one more thing: caring, protecting,
demands goodness, it calls for a certain tenderness.
In the Gospels, Saint Joseph appears as a strong and
courageous man, a working man, yet in his heart we see great
tenderness, which is not the virtue of the weak but rather a
sign of strength of spirit and a capacity for concern,
for compassion, for genuine openness to others, for love.
We must not be afraid of goodness, of tenderness!

In every epoch and in every place blessed are those who, on the strength of the word of God proclaimed in the Church and witnessed by Christians, believe that Jesus Christ is the love of God incarnate, Mercy incarnate. And this applies for each one of us!

The Church is missionary.
Christ sends us forth to
bring the joy of the Gospel
to the whole world.

Christ died and rose once for all, and for everyone, but the power of the Resurrection, this passover from slavery to evil to the freedom of goodness, must be accomplished in every age, in our concrete existence, in our everyday lives. How many deserts, even today, do human beings need to cross! Above all, the desert within, when we have no love for God or neighbor, when we fail to realize that we are guardians of all that the Creator has given us and continues to give us. God's mercy can make even the driest land become a garden, can restore life to dry bones.

When we talk about the environment, about creation, my thoughts go to the first pages of the Bible, to the book of Genesis, where it says that God puts men and women on the earth to till it and keep it (cf. 2:15). And these questions occur to me: What does cultivating and preserving the earth mean? Are we truly cultivating and caring for creation? Or are we exploiting and neglecting it? The verb "cultivate" reminds me of the care a farmer takes to ensure that his land will be productive and that his produce will be shared. What great attention, enthusiasm and dedication! Cultivating and caring for creation is an instruction of God which he gave not only at the beginning of history, but has also given to each one of us; it is part of his plan; it means making the world increase with responsibility, transforming it so that it may be a garden, an inhabitable place for us all.

Journeying. "O house of Jacob, come, let us walk in the light of the Lord" (Isaiah 2:5). This is the first thing that God said to Abraham: Walk in my presence and live blamelessly. Journeying: our life is a journey, and when we stop moving, things go wrong. Always journeying, in the presence of the Lord, in the light of the Lord, seeking to live with the blamelessness that God asked of Abraham in his promise.

Historical events almost always demand a nuanced interpretation which at times can also take into account the dimension of faith. Ecclesial events are certainly no more intricate than political or economic events! But they do have one particular underlying feature: they follow a pattern which does not readily correspond to the "worldly" categories which we are accustomed to use, and so it is not easy to interpret and communicate them to a wider and more varied public. The Church is certainly a human and historical institution with all that that entails, yet her nature is not essentially political but spiritual: the Church is the People of God, the Holy People of God making its way to encounter Jesus Christ.

Only from this perspective can a satisfactory account be given of the Church's life and activity.

Christ is the Church's Pastor, but his presence in history passes through the freedom of human beings; from their midst one is chosen to serve as his Vicar, the Successor of the Apostle Peter. Yet Christ remains the center, not the Successor of Peter: Christ, Christ is the center...

... Christ is the fundamental point of reference, the heart of the Church. Without him, Peter and the Church would not exist or have reason to exist. As Benedict XVI frequently reminded us, Christ is present in Church and guides her.

The Spirit of the Risen Christ drove out fear from the Apostles' hearts and impelled them to leave the Upper Rome in order to spread the Gospel. Let us too have greater courage in witnessing to our faith in the Risen Christ!

The Christian life is a militant one, presupposing a struggle,
but "our battle is not against flesh and blood creatures but against
principalities and powers, against the rulers of this world of
darkness, against the evil spirits that inhabit the celestial regions"
(Ephesians 6:12). Weapons made to our measure do not help us
win this struggle; we need the "armor of God" in order to
"resist and remain on our feet on the evil day after having
overcome every trial"; and the weapon of God is the CROSS.
On it, wickedness was conquered once and for all.

This is beautiful and important for us Christians: to meet on Sundays, to greet each other, to speak to each other as we are doing now, in the square.
A square which, thanks to the media, has global dimensions.

To initiate love is a labor
of craftsmen, of patient
individuals, of persons who
spend everything they have
to persuade, to listen,
to draw nearer.
And this craftsman's labor
has peaceful and magic
creators of love.

57

From the beauty of all these liturgical things, which is not so much about trappings and fine fabrics than about the glory of our God resplendent in his people, alive and strengthened, we turn now to a consideration of activity, action...

... The precious oil which anoints the head of Aaron does more than simply lend fragrance to his person; it overflows down to "the edges." The Lord will say this clearly: his anointing is meant for the poor, prisoners and the sick, for those who are sorrowing and alone. My dear brothers, the ointment is not intended just to make us fragrant, much less to be kept in a jar, for then it would become rancid ... and the heart bitter.

Let us keep the faith we have received and which is our true treasure, let us renew our faithfulness to the Lord, even in the midst of obstacles and misunderstanding. God will never let us lack strength and calmness.

One of the titles of the Bishop of Rome is Pontiff, that is,
a builder of bridges with God and between people.
My wish is that the dialogue between us should help to
build bridges connecting all people, in such a way that
everyone can see in the other not an enemy, not a rival, but
a brother or sister to be welcomed and embraced!
My own origins impel me to work for the building of
bridges. As you know, my family is of Italian origin;
and so this dialogue between places and cultures a great
distance apart matters greatly to me, this dialogue between
one end of the world and the other, which today are
growing ever closer, more interdependent, more in need
of opportunities to meet and to create real spaces
of authentic fraternity.

Like the Apostles at the Last Supper, a Church that preaches must always begin with prayer, with asking for the flame of the Holy Spirit. Only a faithful and intense rapport with God allows us to leave behind our own constraints and to proclaim the Gospel with parresia. *Without prayer our actions become empty and our proclamation has no spirit and is not animated by the Spirit.*

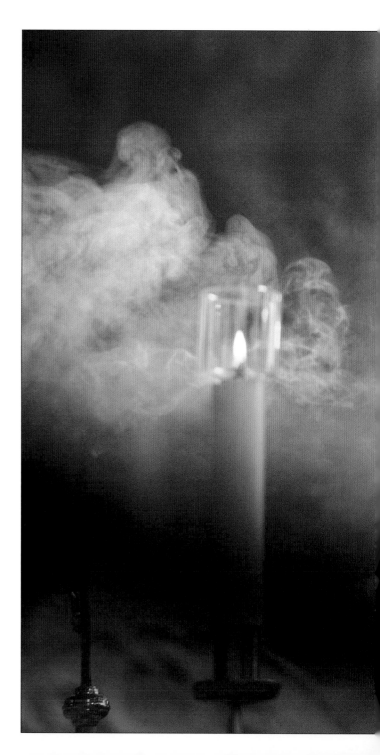

Building. Building the Church. We speak of stones: stones are solid; but living stones, stones anointed by the Holy Spirit. Building the Church, the Bride of Christ, on the cornerstone that is the Lord himself.

This is another kind of movement in our lives: building.

66

The Church is sent by the Risen Christ to pass on to men and women the forgiveness of sins and thereby make the Kingdom of love grow, to sow peace in hearts so that they may also be strengthened in relationships, in every society, in institutions.

We ought to know that
to be a good Christian it
is necessary to realize that
we are sinners. If any one
of us does not realize that
he is a sinner, then he
is not a good Christian.
That is the first condition.
But a real sinner: "I am a
sinner for this reason, for
that other one, for yet that
other one, and so on."
This is the first condition
needed to follow Jesus.

71

One of the more serious temptations that distances us from our contact with the Lord is the awareness of defeat. Before a faith that is combative by definition, the enemy, the evil angel who transforms himself into an angel of light, sows the seeds of pessimism. No one can undertake a battle without first trusting fully in his triumph...

... Who sets out without this conviction loses half
the battle in advance. Christian triumph is always
a cross, but a cross that is a standard of victory.

Jesus does not want to act alone, he came to bring the love of God into the world and he wants to spread it in the style of communion, in the style of brotherhood.
That is why he immediately forms a community of disciples, which is a missionary community. He trains them straight away for the mission, to go forth...

... But pay attention: their purpose is not to socialize, to spend time together, no, their purpose is to proclaim the Kingdom of God, and this is urgent! And it is still urgent today! There is no time to be lost in gossip, there is no need to wait for everyone's consensus, what is necessary is to go out and proclaim.
To all people you bring the peace of Christ, and if they do not welcome it, you go ahead just the same. To the sick you bring healing, because God wants to heal man of every evil.

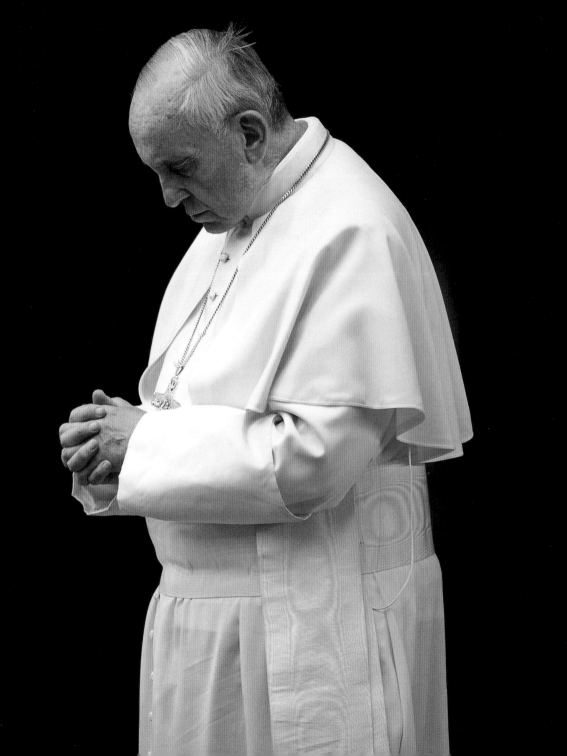

Here is the first word that I wish to say to you: joy!
Do not be men and women of sadness: a Christian can never be sad!
Never give way to discouragement! Ours is not a joy born of having
many possessions, but from having encountered a Person: Jesus, in our
midst; it is born from knowing that with him we are never alone, even
at difficult moments, even when our life's journey comes up against
problems and obstacles that seem insurmountable [...] he accompanies
us and carries us on his shoulders. This is our joy.

No one is the most important person in the Church, we are all equal in God's eyes. Some of you might say "Listen, Mr. Pope, you are not our equal." Yes, I am like each one of you. We are all equal, we are brothers and sisters! No one is anonymous: we all both constitute and build the Church. This also invites us to reflect on the fact that if the brick of our Christian life goes missing, the beauty of the Church loses something. Some people say "I have nothing to do with the Church"; but in this way the brick of a life in this beautiful Temple is left out. No one can go away; we must all bring the Church our life, our heart, our love, our thought and our work: all of us together.

Unfortunately, efforts have often been made to blur faith in the Resurrection of Jesus and doubts have crept in, even among believers. It is a little like that "rosewater" faith, as we say; it is not a strong faith. And this is due to superficiality and sometimes to indifference, busy as we are with a thousand things considered more important than faith, or because we have a view of life that is solely horizontal.

However, it is the Resurrection itself that opens us to greater hope, for it opens our life and the life of the world to the eternal future of God, to full happiness, to the certainty that evil, sin and death may be overcome. And this leads to living daily situations with greater trust, to facing them with courage and determination. Christ's Resurrection illuminates these everyday situations with a new light.

The Resurrection of Christ is our strength!

The dignity and importance of work.
The book of Genesis tells us that God created man and woman
entrusting them with the task of filling the earth and subduing it,
which does not mean exploiting it but nurturing and protecting it,
caring for it through their work (cf. Genesis 1:28; 2:15).
Work is part of God's loving plan: we are called to cultivate and care
for all the goods of creation and in this way share in the work
of creation! Work is fundamental to the dignity of a person.
Work, to use a metaphor, "anoints" us with dignity, fills us with
dignity, makes us similar to God, who has worked and still works,
who always acts (cf. John 5:17); it gives one the ability to maintain
oneself, one's family, to contribute to the growth of one's own
nation. And here I think of the difficulties which, in various
countries, today afflict the world of work and business today; I am
thinking of how many, and not only young people, are unemployed,
often due to a purely economic conception of society, which seeks
profit selfishly, beyond the parameters of social justice.

God does not wait for us to go to him but it is he who moves towards us, without calculation, without quantification.
That is what God is like.
He always takes the first step, he comes towards us.

When the food was shared
fairly, with solidarity, no
one was deprived of what he
needed, every community
could meet the needs of its
poorest members. Human and
environmental ecology
go hand in hand.

*Today we have more martyrs than in the first centuries!
However, there is also daily martyrdom, which may not entail
death but is still a "loss of life" for Christ, by doing one's duty
with love, according to the logic of Jesus, the logic of gift, of
sacrifice. Let us think: how many dads and moms every day
put their faith into practice by offering up their own lives in
a concrete way for the good of the family! Think about this!
How many priests, brothers and sisters carry out their service
generously for the Kingdom of God! How many young people
renounce their own interests in order to dedicate themselves
to children, the disabled, the elderly.... They are martyrs too!
Daily martyrs, martyrs of everyday life!*

I would like to ask you: have you sometimes heard the Lord's voice,
in a desire, in a worry? Did he invite you to follow him more closely?
Have you heard him? I can't hear you? There! Have you wanted to
be apostles of Jesus? We must bet on youth for the great ideals.
Do you think this? Do you agree?...

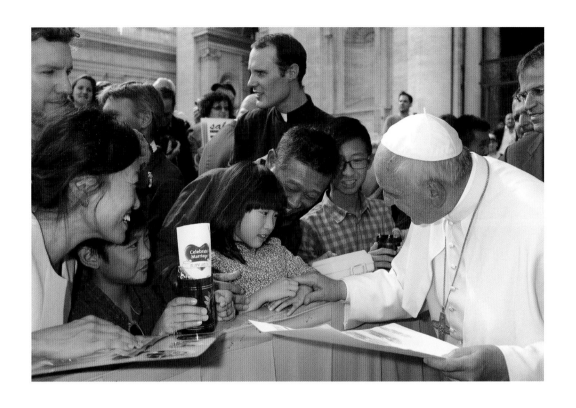

... Ask Jesus what he wants of you and be brave! Be brave! Ask him this! Behind and before every vocation to the priesthood or to the consecrated life there is always the strong and intense prayer of someone: a grandmother, a grandfather, a mother, a father, a community...

*The truth is not grasped
as a thing, the truth is
encountered. It is not
a possession, it is an
encounter with a Person.*

Governing is an art... that can be learned. It is also a science... that can be studied. It is a job... that demands commitment, power, and tenacity. But it is first and foremost a mystery... that cannot always be explained with logical reason.

*We cannot become starched Christians, those over-
educated Christians who speak of theological matters
as they calmly sip their tea.
No! We must become courageous Christians and go
in search of the people who are the very flesh of Christ,
those who are the flesh of Christ!*

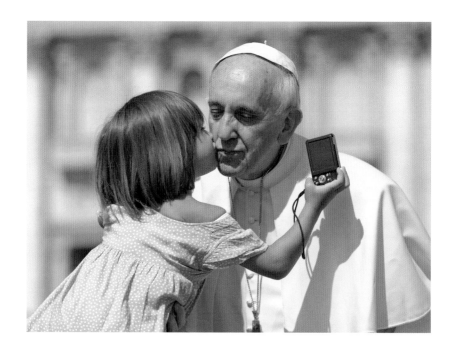

Jesus wants to establish with his friends a relationship which mirrors his own relationship with the Father: a relationship of reciprocal belonging in full trust, in intimate communion. To express this profound understanding, this relationship of friendship, Jesus uses the image of the shepherd with his sheep: he calls them and they recognize his voice, they respond to his call and follow him.

Jesus has no house, because his house is the people, it is we who are his dwelling place, his mission is to open God's doors to all, to be the presence of God's love.

The humble have nothing to lose; on the contrary, to them the road is revealed (cf. Matthew 11:25–26). It is well to recall that this is not the time of payback, of triumph, of accumulation; that in our culture the enemy has sown discord with the Lord's wheat; and that the two grow together. This is not the time to grow habituated but to bend down and gather the five rocks for David's sling (cf. 1 Samuel 17:40). This is the time for prayer.

Evangelizing is the Church's mission. It is not the mission of only a few, but it is mine, yours and our mission.

The Church grows through attraction, thanks to witnesses,
not through proselytizing. Our Christian conversion must
be a grateful response to the marvelous mystery of God's love,
which works through the death and resurrection of the Son and
is presented in every birth to the life of faith, to every pardon
that renews and heals us, in every Eucharist that sows the same
awareness of Christ in us.

The first witnesses of the Resurrection were women. And this is beautiful. This is part of the mission of women; of mothers, of women! Witnessing to their children, to their grandchildren, that Jesus is alive, is living, is risen. Mothers and women, carry on witnessing to this! It is the heart that counts for God, how open to him we are, whether we are like trusting children. However this also makes us think about how women, in the Church and on the journey of faith, had and still have today a special role in opening the doors to the Lord, in following him and in communicating his Face, for the gaze of faith is always in need of the simple and profound gaze of love. The Apostles and disciples find it harder to believe. The women, not so. Peter runs to the tomb but stops at the empty tomb; Thomas has to touch the wounds on Jesus' body with his hands. On our way of faith it is also important to know and to feel that God loves us and not to be afraid to love him. Faith is professed with the lips and with the heart, with words and with love.

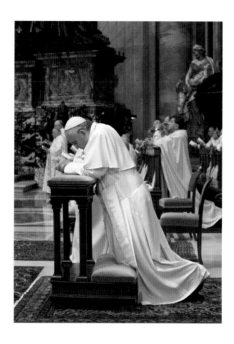

The Church invites everyone to be embraced by the Father's
tenderness and forgiveness.

It is hard to forgive others. Lord, grant us your mercy,
so that we can always forgive.

*It is no longer man who commands, but money, money, cash
commands. And God our Father gave us the task of protecting the
earth – not for money, but for ourselves: for men and women.
We have this task! Nevertheless men and women are sacrificed to the
idols of profit and consumption: it is the "culture of waste."
If a computer breaks it is a tragedy, but poverty, the needs and dramas
of so many people end up being considered normal.*

*If on a winter's night, here on the Via Ottaviano – for example
– someone dies, that is not news. If there are children in so many
parts of the world who have nothing to eat, that is not news, it seems
normal. It cannot be so! And yet these things enter into normality:
that some homeless people should freeze to death on the street – this
doesn't make news. On the contrary, when the stock market drops 10
points in some cities, it constitutes a tragedy. Someone who dies is
not news, but lowering income by 10 points is a tragedy!
In this way people are thrown aside as if they were trash.*

*Thirdly, professing. We can walk as much as we want,
we can build many things, but if we do not profess Jesus Christ,
things go wrong. We may become a charitable NGO, but not the
Church, the Bride of the Lord.
When we are not walking, we stop moving...*

... When we are not building on the stones, what happens?
The same thing that happens to children on the beach when they build
sandcastles: everything is swept away, there is no solidity.
When we do not profess Jesus Christ, the saying of Léon Bloy comes
to mind: "Anyone who does not pray to the Lord prays to the devil."
When we do not profess Jesus Christ, we profess the worldliness of the
devil, a demonic worldliness.

A prayer that does not lead you to practical action for your brother – the poor, the sick, those in need of help, a brother in difficulty – is a sterile and incomplete prayer.
But, in the same way, when ecclesial service is attentive only to doing, things gain in importance, functions, structures, and we forget the centrality of Christ. When time is not set aside for dialogue with him in prayer, we risk serving ourselves and not God present in our needy brother and sister.

We need to keep alive in our world the thirst for the absolute, and to counter the dominance of a one-dimensional vision of the human person, a vision which reduces human beings to what they produce and to what they consume: this is one of the most insidious temptations of our time.

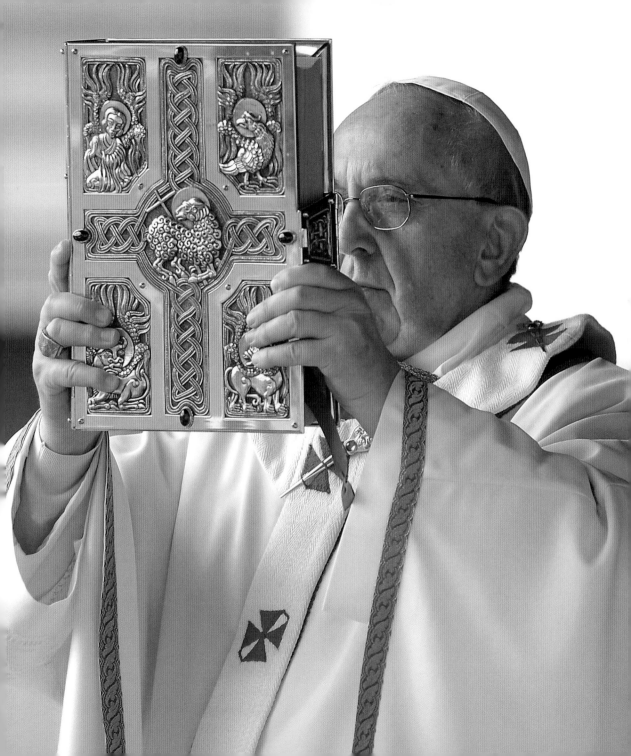

Peace in the whole world, still divided by greed looking for easy gain, wounded by the selfishness which threatens human life and the family, selfishness that continues in human trafficking, the most extensive form of slavery in this twenty-first century! Peace to the whole world, torn apart by violence linked to drug trafficking and by the iniquitous exploitation of natural resources! Peace to this our Earth!

Body and limb, in order to live, must be united!
Unity is superior to conflict, always! Conflicts, if not properly
resolved, divide us from each other, separate us from God.
Conflict can help us to grow, but it can also divide us.
Let us not go down the path of division, of fighting among ourselves!
All united, all united in our differences, but united, always:
this is the way of Jesus. Unity is superior to conflict.
Unity is a grace for which we must ask the Lord that he may liberate
us from the temptation of division, of conflict between us,
of selfishness, of gossip. How much evil gossip does, how much evil!
Never gossip about others, never!
So much damage to the Church comes from division among
Christians, from biases, from narrow interests.

The temptation to set God aside in order to put ourselves at the center is always at the door, and the experience of sin injures our Christian life, our being children of God. For this reason we must have the courage of faith not to allow ourselves to be guided by the mentality that tells us: "God is not necessary, he is not important for you," and so forth. It is exactly the opposite: only by behaving as children of God, without despairing at our shortcomings, at our sins, only by feeling loved by him will our life be new, enlivened by serenity and joy. God is our strength! God is our hope!

Today, it is important not to turn in on ourselves, burying our own talent, our spiritual, intellectual, and material riches, everything that the Lord has given us, but, rather to open ourselves, to be supportive, to be attentive to others. In the square I have seen that there are many young people here: it is true, isn't it? Are there many young people? Where are they? I ask you who are just setting out on your journey through life: have you thought about the talents that God has given you? Have you thought of how you can put them at the service of others? Do not bury your talents! Set your stakes on great ideals, the ideals that enlarge the heart, the ideals of service that make your talents fruitful. Life is not given to us to be jealously guarded for ourselves, but is given to us so that we may give it in turn. Dear young people, have a deep spirit! Do not be afraid to dream of great things!

Jesus does not force you to be a Christian. But if you say you are a Christian, you must believe that Jesus has the power — the only one who has the power — to renew the world, to renew your life, to renew your family, to renew the community, to renew everybody.

This is the message that we should bear with us today, asking the Father to allow us to be submissive to the inspiration of the Spirit who does this work: the Spirit of Jesus.

*The absence of love, its vulgarization and permanent degradation,
even beginning with some pseudo-religious discourses, not only
dehumanizes but also ultimately depoliticizes us. Love, on the
other hand, hastens to care for that which is common and above all
for the common good that strengthens and favors particular goods.*

Our God is a God who draws near. A God who makes himself near. A God who began to walk with his people and later made himself one with his people in Jesus Christ in order to make himself close.

*When the Church is closed, she falls sick, she falls sick.
Think of a room that has been closed for a year. When you go
into it there is a smell of dampness, many things are wrong
with it. A Church closed in on herself is the same, a sick
Church. The Church must step outside herself. To go where?
Towards the outskirts of existence, whatever they may be.*

To cross the threshold of faith is to act, to have faith in the power of the Holy Spirit, which is present in the Church and which also manifests itself in the signs of the times; it is to accompany the continuous movement of life and history without succumbing to a paralyzing defeatism in which the past is always better than the present. It is urgent to think about the new, to generate the new, to create the new, kneading life with the new leavening of justice and sanctity (1 Corinthians 5:8).

Who were those who believed without seeing?
Other disciples, other men and women of Jerusalem, who, on the
testimony of the Apostles and the women, believed, even though they
had not met the Risen Jesus. This is a very important word about faith,
we can call it the beatitude of faith.
Blessed are those who have not seen but have believed:
this is the beatitude of faith!

Christ has fully triumphed over evil once and for all, but it is up to us,
to the people of every epoch, to welcome this victory into our life and
into the actual situations of history and society...

... For this reason it seems to me important to emphasize what we ask God today in the liturgy. "O God, who gives constant increase/to your Church by new offspring,/grant that your servants may hold fast in their lives/to the Sacrament they have received in faith."

Our God who lives in
the city and implicates
himself in everyday life
neither discriminates nor
relativizes. His truth is
that of the encounter that
perceives different faces,
yet each of these faces
is unique.

God thinks like the Samaritan who did not pass by the unfortunate man, pitying him or looking at him from the other side of the road, but helped him without asking for anything in return; without asking whether he was a Jew, a pagan or a Samaritan, whether he was rich or poor: he asked for nothing. He went to help him: God is like this.
God thinks like the shepherd who lays down his life in order to defend and save his sheep.

*Please, I would like to ask all those who have positions of
responsibility in economic, political and social life, and
all men and women of goodwill: let us be "protectors"
of creation, protectors of God's plan inscribed in nature,
protectors of one another and of the environment.
Let us not allow omens of destruction and death
to accompany the advance of this world!
But to be "protectors," we also have to keep watch over
ourselves! Let us not forget that hatred, envy and pride
defile our lives! Being protectors, then, also means keeping
watch over our emotions, over our hearts, because they are
the seat of good and evil intentions: intentions that build up
and tear down!
We must not be afraid of goodness or even tenderness!*

Jesus wants us to be Christians, freely as he was, with the freedom which comes from this dialogue with the Father, from this dialogue with God. Jesus does not want selfish Christians who follow their own ego, who do not talk to God. Nor does he want weak Christians, Christians who have no will of their own, "remote-controlled" Christians incapable of creativity, who always seek to connect with the will of someone else and are not free.

Jesus wants us free. And where is this freedom created?

It is created in dialogue with God in the person's own conscience. If a Christian is unable to speak with God, if he cannot hear God in his own conscience, he is not free, he is not free. This is why we must learn to listen to our conscience more.

Why can this water quench our thirst deep down?
We know that water is essential to life; without water we die;
it quenches, washes, makes the earth fertile.
In the Letter to the Romans we find these words: "God's love
has been poured into our hearts through the Holy Spirit who has
been given to us" (5:5). The "living water," the Holy Spirit, the
Gift of the Risen One who dwells in us, purifies us, illuminates
us, renews us, transforms us because he makes us participants in
the very life of God that is Love.
That is why the Apostle Paul says that the Christian's life is
moved by the Holy Spirit and by his fruit, which is "love, joy,
peace, patience, kindness, goodness, faithfulness, gentleness,
self-control."

The Most Holy Trinity is not the product of human reasoning but the face with which God actually revealed himself, not from the heights of a throne, but walking with humanity. It is Jesus himself who revealed the Father to us and who promised us the Holy Spirit. God walked with his people in the history of the People of Israel and Jesus has always walked with us and promised us the Holy Spirit who is fire, who teaches us everything we do not know and from within us guides us, gives us good ideas and good inspirations.

The look of faith grows
each time we set the
Word into practice.
Contemplation improves
with action.

Well, the problem is that we ourselves tire, we do not want to ask, we grow weary of asking for forgiveness. He never tires of forgiving, but at times we get tired of asking for forgiveness. Let us never tire, let us never tire! He is the loving Father who always pardons, who has that heart of mercy for us all. And let us too learn to be merciful to everyone.

Only the laborer who has learned how to renounce vain ambition, sloth, and inconstancy in order to devote himself to pastoral service each and every day, only he will understand the price of Christ's redemption in his heart, and — perhaps without articulating it clearly — his hardworking hands will protect and enhance the unity of the Church, this togetherness with God that originates with membership in the Holy Mother Church, which makes us children of the Father, brothers among ourselves, and fathers of God's people.

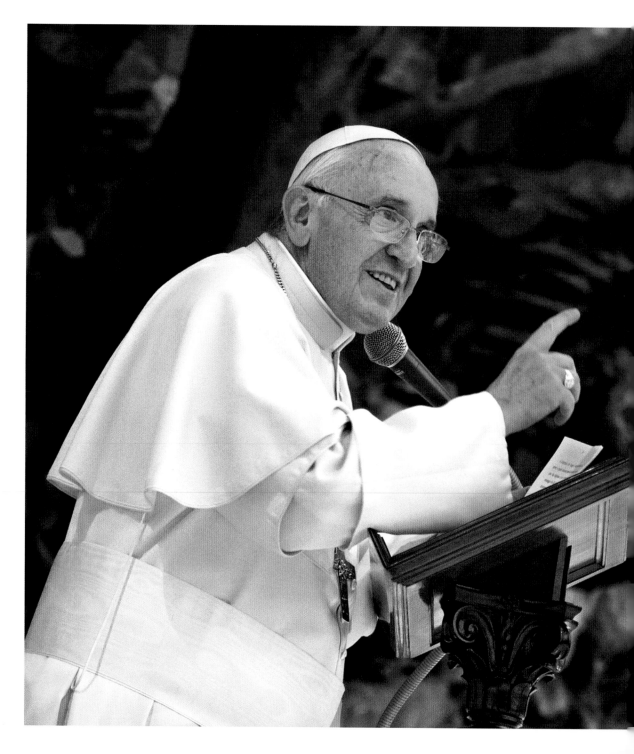

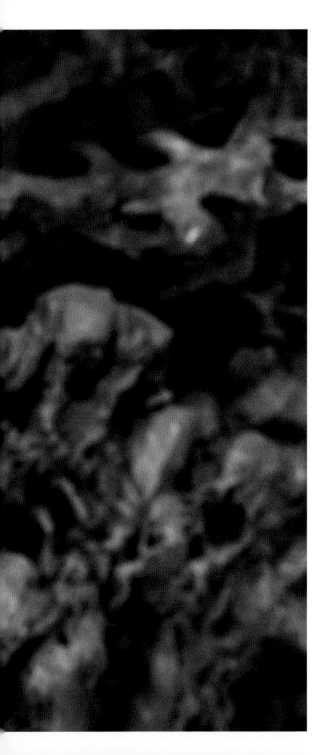

Fighting poverty, both material and spiritual, building peace and constructing bridges: these, as it were, are the reference points for a journey that I want to invite each of the countries here represented to take up. But it is a difficult journey, if we do not learn to grow in love for this world of ours.

I wish to extend an invitation to solidarity to everyone,
and I would like to encourage those in public office to make every
effort to give new impetus to employment, this means caring for the
dignity of the person, but above all I would say do not lose hope.
St. Joseph also experienced moments of difficulty, but he never lost
faith and was able to overcome them, in the certainty that
God never abandons us.

And when we say "home" we mean a place of hospitality,
a dwelling, a pleasant environment where one stays readily, finds
oneself, feels inserted into a territory, in a community.
Yet more profoundly, "home" is a word with a typically familiar
flavor, which recalls warmth, affection, the love that can be felt in
a family. Hence the "home" represents the most precious human
treasures, that of encounter, that of relations among people,
different in age, culture and history, but who live together and
together help one another to grow.
For this reason, the "home" is a crucial place in life, where life grows
and can be fulfilled, because it is a place in which every person
learns to receive love and to give love.
This is "home."

People's memory is not a computer but a heart.
People, like Mary, keep things in their heart.
In this sense, Spain has taught us to make a solid covenant and
to remember faithfully the Lord, His Mother and the saints,
founding on them the spiritual unity of our nations.
Because memory is a power that unifies and integrates.
Just as intelligence left to its own devices grows corrupt,
so memory is the vital nucleus of a family or country.
A family without memory does not deserve to be defined as such.
A family that does not respect or honor its aged members, who are
its living memory, is a broken family; but a family and a people
that remember are a family and a people that have a future.

In the Church, but also in society, a key word of which we must not be frightened is "solidarity," that is, the ability to make what we have, our humble capacities, available to God, for only in sharing, in giving, will our life be fruitful. Solidarity is a word seen badly by the spirit of the world!

My wish is that all of us, after these days of grace,
will have the courage, yes, the courage, to walk in the
presence of the Lord, with the Lord's Cross; to build
the Church on the Lord's blood which was poured out
on the Cross; and to profess the one glory:
Christ crucified.
And in this way, the Church will go forward.

Work is part of God's loving plan, we are called to
cultivate and care for all the goods of creation and
in this way share in the work of creation!
Work is fundamental to the dignity of a person.

As you know, there are various reasons why I chose the name of Francis of Assisi, a familiar figure far beyond the borders of Italy and Europe, even among those who do not profess the Catholic faith. One of the first reasons was Francis' love for the poor. How many poor people there still are in the world! And what great suffering they have to endure! After the example of Francis of Assisi, the Church in every corner of the globe has always tried to care for and look after those who suffer from want, and I think that in many of your countries you can attest to the generous activity of Christians who dedicate themselves to helping the sick, orphans, the homeless and all the marginalized, thus striving to make society more humane and more just.

I would like to speak especially to you
young people: be committed to your
daily duties, your studies,
your work, to relationships
of friendship, to helping others;
your future also depends on how you
live these precious years of your life.
Do not be afraid of commitment,
of sacrifice and do not view the
future with fear.
Keep your hope alive: there is always
a light on the horizon.

*Always convey the power
of the Gospel!
Do not be afraid!
Always feel joy
and enthusiasm for
communion in the
Church! May the
Risen Lord be with you
constantly and may Our
Lady protect you!*

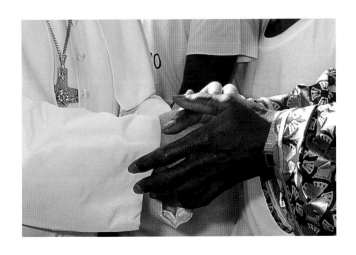

The challenge of being a citizen, in addition to being an anthropological fact, is framed within the horizon of the political arena. This, in fact, is a matter of the call and energy of the good, which spreads to sociable friendship. And it is not a matter of an "abstract idea of the good," of a theoretical reflection based on a vague concept of ethics, and "ethicism," but on an idea that develops in the energy of goodness, in the very nature of the person, in his or her disposition.

Old age is – as I like to say – the seat of life's wisdom.
The old have acquired the wisdom that comes from having journeyed
through life, like the old man Simeon, the old prophetess Anna in the
Temple. And that wisdom enabled them to recognize Jesus.
Let us pass on this wisdom to the young: like good wine that improves
with age, let us give life's wisdom to the young...

...I am reminded of a German poet who said of old age:
Es is ruhig, das Alter, und fromm: *it is a time of*
tranquillity and prayer. And also a time to pass on
this wisdom to the young.

We are all called to be friends with Jesus.
Don't be afraid to love the Lord.

Let's try to be open to God's word, and open
to the Lord's surprises when he speaks to us.

When someone is summoned
by the judge or is involved in
legal proceedings, the first thing
he does is to seek a lawyer to
defend him. We have One who
always defends us, who defends
us from the snares of the devil,
who defends us from ourselves
and from our sins!
Dear brothers and sisters, we
have this Advocate; let us not be
afraid to turn to him to ask for
forgiveness, to ask for a blessing,
to ask for mercy! He always
pardons us. He is our Advocate:
he always defends us!
Don't forget this!

We must recover the whole sense of gift, of gratuitousness, of solidarity.
Rampant capitalism has taught the logic of profit at all costs, of giving to get,
of exploitation without looking at the person... and we see the results in the
crisis we are experiencing! This Home is a place that teaches charity,
a "school" of charity, which instructs me to go encounter every person,
not for profit, but for love. The music — let us call it — of this Home is love.

Dear brothers and sisters, being the Church, to be the people of God, in accordance with the Father's great design of love, means to be the leaven of God in this humanity of ours. It means to proclaim and to bring God's salvation to this world of ours, so often led astray, in need of answers that give courage, hope and new vigor for the journey.

May the Church be a place of God's mercy and hope, where all feel welcomed, loved, forgiven and encouraged to live according to the good life of the Gospel. And to make others feel welcomed, loved, forgiven and encouraged, the Church must be with doors wide open so that all may enter. And we must go out through these doors and proclaim the Gospel.

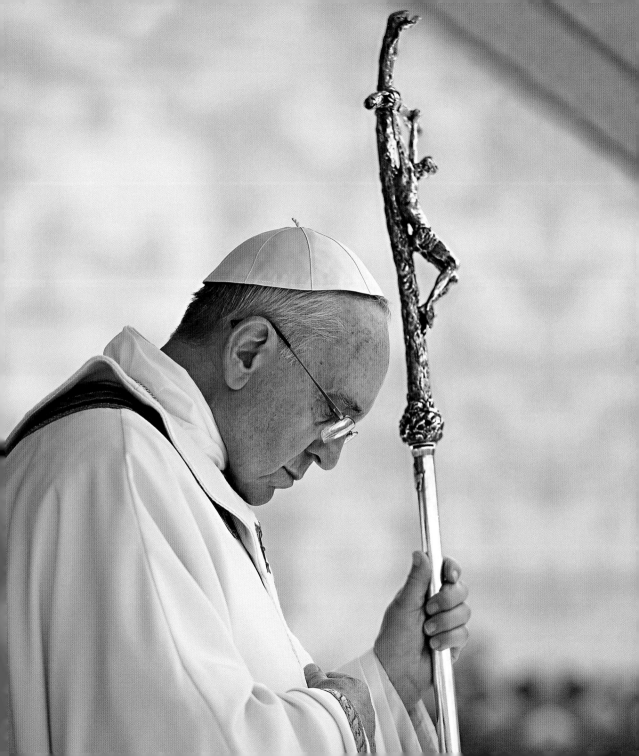

He who avoids conflict cannot be a citizen because he does not take it on himself. He is an inhabitant who washes his hands in the face of daily conflicts.

*Labor is the face of dignity
and the pillar that carries
personal and social identity.
The subjective dimension of
labor is a fundamental axis
for recognizing and assessing
people's contribution to the
process of production and the
construction of a narrative.*

*Man of every time and place desires a full and beautiful life,
just and good, a life that is not threatened by death, but can
still mature and grow to fullness...*

... Man is like a traveler who, crossing the deserts of life,
thirsts for the living water that is gushing and fresh, capable
of quenching his deep desire for light, love, beauty and peace.
We all feel this desire!

*Jesus lived the daily reality of the most ordinary people:
he was moved as he faced the crowd that seemed like a flock without
a shepherd; he wept before the sorrow that Martha and Mary felt
at the death of their brother, Lazarus; he called a publican to be his
disciple; he also suffered betrayal by a friend.
In him God has given us the certitude that he is with us, he is
among us. "Foxes," he, Jesus, said, "have holes, and birds of the air
have nests, but the Son of man has nowhere to lay his head"
(Matthew 8:20). Jesus has no house, because his house is the people,
it is we who are his dwelling place, his mission is to open God's
doors to all, to be the presence of God's love.*

Citizens *constitute a logical category. The People constitute a historical and mythical category. We live in society, and this we all understand and express with logic. The People cannot be explained solely in a logical manner. They contain additional meaning that escapes us if we do not resort to other modes of comprehension and other forms of logic and hermeneutics. The challenge of being a citizen involves living and manifesting oneself in two forms of belonging: belonging to* society *and belonging to a* people. *One lives in society and depends on a people.*

*Youth! Dear young people, I saw you in the
procession as you were coming in;
I think of you celebrating around Jesus, waving your olive
branches. I think of you crying out his name and expressing
your joy at being with him! You have an important part in
the celebration of faith!*

... You bring us the joy of faith and you tell us that we must live the faith with a young heart, always: a young heart, even at the age of seventy or eighty. Dear young people! With Christ, the heart never grows old! Yet all of us, all of you know very well that the King whom we follow and who accompanies us is very special: he is a King who loves even to the Cross and who teaches us to serve and to love.

History is created by successive generations of a people
on a course. For this reason every individual effort
(however precious)
every phase of a rotating government
(however significant it may be)
as well as the events and the historical processes that
in the course of time forge the history of a people
— the conveyor of life and culture —
are no more than parts of "a complex and diverse
whole that interacts over time";
people fight for a destiny, fight to live with dignity.

The grand diplomacy that has granted so many fruits to the Church feeds on charity and penance. One of the traits of this community, which today joins together to celebrate, is its closeness to the periphery of existence, to the very poorest, to the most marginalized, to the most foresaken. Perhaps, as in the case of Jesus, it is from this very closeness that it draws the power to abase itself and advance the craftsman's duty to pacify, approach and initiate love.

GIUSEPPE COSTA (1946: GELA, ITALY)

A Salesian priest and journalist, Giuseppe Costa began his work in schools and with youth animation. He specialized in Pastoral Theology at the Pontifical Salesian University in Rome and completed a master's in Journalism at Marquette University (Wisconsin, USA). Costa, a visiting lecturer in Journalism and Publishing at the Pontifical Salesian University, taught at the University of Catania and the Luiss in Rome. Since 2007, he has been in charge of the Vatican Publishing House and was nominated Counselor of the Pontifical Council for Social Communications. His numerous publications include: *Parole attorno ai media* (Sciascia, 2002), *Dentro la fotografia* (Edizioni della Meridiana, 2002), *Dietro il giornale* (Las, 2004), *Editoria, media e religione* (Lev, 2009). He collaborated with Franco Zangrilli and published *Giornalismo e Letteratura* (Sciascia, 2005); with Angelo Paoluzi he cowrote *Giornalismo. Teoria e pratica* (Las, 2006), and *Giornalismo e Religione* (Lev, 2012).

Acknowledgments

The author thanks Dr. Francesca Angeletti and
Mrs. Maria Luisa Marino for their knowledgeable collaboration.

POPE
FRANCIS

THOUGHTS
and WORDS
for the SOUL